Thoughts on Traditional Korean Literature

Based on Translated Works by Kevin O'Rourke

Rowena Kong

2022

Copyright © 2022 by Rowena Kong

All rights reserved. This book or any portion thereof may not be reproduced or used in any manner whatsoever without the express written permission of the publisher except for the use of brief quotations in a book review or scholarly journal.

First Printing: 2022

Contents

Yi Kyubo 4

Chong Chisang 7

Poetry of Later Choson Dynasty 10

Literature: The Tale of Shim Ch'ong and Tears of Blood 14

Yi Kyubo

Yi Kyubo (O'Rourke, 2006) was one of the greatest poets who lived during the Koryo period in traditional Korea. He was also one who faced many challenges and setbacks during his career in a turbulent era of the kingdom. Nonetheless, he still managed to produce many of the best poems in Korean literature history. His poems not only engage the reader concerning down-to-earth intricate details of everyday life, but also teach and admonish the aspiring young poets of his day on the significance of meaningful content above decorative form. The subtlety and details of content in his *hanshi* poems connect nicely with each other with rich rhetorical devices and an interplay of contrasts and comparisons frequently used in traditional East-Asian literary works. Yi cleverly hid moral message underneath telling of events and processes of nature in his works. The poems progress in a steady and calm rhythm that keeps the reader engaged with interest. There are somewhat a distinct style and expressions that appeared not done in haste and flow with ease and consistency - such could denote his liberal and nonchalant or indeliberate attitude in life. Interestingly, there is a good choice of attention-grabbing themes in his poems which could even relate to the questionable morals of our modern age. No doubt, Yi had persistence in upholding morals and offering worthwhile lessons in spite of the many unheeding poets of his day. It can be observed that the poet cherished children and family members and his poems spoke fondly in detail of precious familial relationships and interaction - other poets had not expressed to such realistic and candid level that modern East-Asian families can relate with. There is an implication of application and parallelism with the present age - valuing meaningful content above form in poetry is like valuing inner conscience above superficial materialism in our modern world.

Works: "Evening on the Mountain: Song to the Moon in the Well (1) & (2)," "On the Road: Hearing the Sounds of *Paduk* Stones in a Pavilion," "View from my Straw Hut" and "On Poetry"

"Evening on the Mountain: Song to the Moon in the Well (1) & (2)"

This pair of poems teach moral lesson through cultural and religious channels, i.e. the moon and Buddhist monk, water, jar and well as representations of the practical reality of daily life. They both highlight the similar covert desires of common people and religious monks. Both the "golden mirror" reflection of the moon and water have clarity in appearance and so could function similarly as a "mirror." These "mirrors" appear to reflect the inner desires of men, instead of physical mirrors which reflect the outward facial appearances. The first poem ended on a more positive note as the speaker returned home with "half" of the new moon instead of spilling "all" the moon in the case of the mountain monk(2), implying that the moon is more "merciful" towards a wishful common person than a covetous monk.

They also effectively condensed the drama of a moral and philosophical lesson into just four lines - the monk's reverie with the moon, his decisive action on such thoughts and dream, followed by a counter-action, i.e. reaching and returning to temple that demanded a contrasting shift in thought and action, and finally learning the moral of the lesson. With its feature of the moon and well that hold cultural and aesthetic prominence in the Eastern world, this *hanshi* paints a moving picture of anticipation that ultimately ended in loss and return to the plain reality of emptiness, causing the reader to feel for the speaker at its conclusion, thus inducing a certain level of mood and emotional reaction from the reader.

"On the Road: Hearing the Sounds of *Paduk* Stones in a Pavilion"

From the bamboo curtains and indistinct shadows, Yi showed the blurring of distinction between the players, whether in terms of identity, clan or class, and forsaking the spirit of ambitious competition and people division for pure leisurely pleasure and enjoyment of one another's company may overshadow self-consciousness and pride, like the amusing sounds of clinking paduk stones which even children may find pleasurable in listening. Such may relate to Yi's liberal worldview and at times, a carefree demeanour. Interestingly, hail after the rain not only produce sounds, but also sentimental beauty and purity in their shape and colour of appearance, hence the speaker is reminded of the beauty in the midst of company with least ill contention.

"View from my Straw Hut"

This fascinating work describes the pure fatherly enjoyment of watching one's young children played about with cute little creatures in the garden while the speaker gradually drifted to sleep from reading by the corner. Reading and work fell to second place compared to the sheer lasting joy of reveling in parental pleasure of company with his children - a time-defying parallelism with modern parents' love for their children.

"On Poetry"

The seamless flow and mergence of thought and expression as a top-notch quality of poems is a greatly treasured talent, which Yi succeeded in achieving. Nonetheless, compromising worthwhile content with a focused meaning for unnecessarily flowery expressions is like doing away with the nutrition and nourishment of life.

Yi lamented the trend of new poets to do flattering decoration of their works with a loss in essence and meaningful content that have depths in thought. These superficial poems were easier for those poets to compose, like it is easy for men to err than to refrain from wrongdoing. Yi wanted to help restore the former trend of poetry and with the little effort he could manage to contribute, he eagerly did so in spite of his tears and scornful laugh directed at him - a subtle parallelism with modern society in which the majority of people and popular media value and indulge in superficial materialism and secularism without regard for clarity of inner conscience and distinguishing between right and wrong, while the conscientious persisted in silent integrity.

Chong Chisang

Chong Chisang (O'Rourke, 2006) was an ill-fated yet sensible poet who was underappreciated in his days; he was faced with immense challenges and opposition but remained true to his heart, values, principles and native hometown. The poems of this talented figure may be poignant yet imbued with the beauty of emotional depths and expressions that reaches out. A sense of humility in disposition could be subtly perceived from the speaker's voice and thought in his poems. Chong can be said to deeply value relations and friendship that ached "silently" and helplessly from separation. His emotional expressions tend to merge yearning and wistfulness with the beauty of imagery. Chong had a preference for vivid nature river scenes to accompany the flow of his emotions.

Works: "Sending off a Friend," "The Taedong River" and "Tiny Room in Flower Sage Temple"

"Sending off a Friend"

In this poem, Chong chose the imagery of a river, perhaps humbly low lying among green grass of the land, filled with "tears" cried out of separation from a friend, which shows how much he valued closeness and relationships and then the heartfelt aches inflicted by solitude, which bears intertextuality with "The Taedong River." This opens with positive note of green grass and rain clearing and compares with negativity in tears contributing to the waters of the river, hinting in spite of volumes of tears, one's relationship will continue to persist as evergreen as the grass, hopeful that one day, the rain "tears" would be cleared. Was this a mirror to the hidden inner optimism within the poet that could have fueled his undying persistence in voicing out support for his northern Korean hometown? Nevertheless, it indirectly teaches the reader on cherishing relations and the burden of separation, bearing striking intertextuality with "The Taedong River." It is hopeful for a new beginning suffused with life(greenery) and beauty and a juxtaposition of implicit optimism with explicit tears of separation.

"The Taedong River"

It is a reiteration of a sad song as in "Sending off a Friend," yet both are very brief works and never longwinded, hinting a lack of the speaker's heavy indulgence in the song. Again, strong intertextuality with "Sending off a Friend" echoes hope and optimism in the midst of long running tears. On the other hand, these two poems raise a question of whether the poet was really expecting the Taedong river to run dry one day or nothing more than pure intention of poetic expression. Should it run dry, will not the green grass along its long bank lose out on nourishment and beauty? Should it run dry, how long will the dryness last in the event of rainfalls to replenish the water? It appears that the author is still seeing beauty in the midst of tears, evergreen in the midst of separation. Perhaps, a hint that the tears in rain and the deep river water then were worthwhile and having sown, held the promise that they would reap reunion someday, or so Chong thought, and imagined figuratively more than the realism that they would run dry somehow...In spite of such, it is a rich, though brief, imagery of visual nature(colour of green grass and water ripples) and audible stimuli(rain stopping and sad song) , overall well-rounded.

"Tiny Room in Flower Sage Temple"

Here is another work of a rich description of sights of distant temple on high mountains. It emphasises positivity of solitude by "the house with only a few rooms," a contrast with huge palaces. The sacredness of the setting is a want of peace in the country and separation from conflicting royal court affairs. The walls could hint the speaker's admiration of long-standing moral integrity that could withstand the test of time and endured through the process of aging, like his undying loyalty to native land and perseverance against opposition.

Conclusion

Both Yi Kyubo and Chong Chisang were poets who valued relations and candid expressions of inner emotions and thoughts in spite of challenges and setbacks in life. They enjoyed the company of loved ones and close friends, felt the aches of separations and practised humility in the midst of bleak outlook on society. They were poets who aspired for change for the better, whether through their *hanshi* works or in deeds, and persisted with courage 'till the end of their days. It is no wonder they have won the admiration of present-day scholars.

While Yi wrote for a longer span of time to his ripe old age and consequently had many works credited, Chong had the essence of youth, determination and endurance, perhaps a testimony to withstand forces of opposition, under the tone of his poems. If Yi can be lauded as the poet of an elder's wisdom, then Chong can be described as the poet of undaunted youth. Overall, both were game-changers in their times and marked transitions in the history of not only Korean literature, but its culture as well.

Poetry of Later Choson Dynasty

The genre of poetry from Later Choson is in certain ways connected with the backdrop of the political and societal climate environments of the period, which were not without turbulent events and transitional stages in which the educated elites and commoners who were increasingly class-conscious participated fully. It could be that there came to be a greater exchange of communication between classes, i.e. elite officials and lesser educated common people, but whether inter-class understanding of each other deepened is open to question. Hanshi and sasol shijo both have their distinct characteristics which appeal, yet they were composed by and foremost targeted at different classes of people. Hanshi possesses rich rhetorical devices, motivation to compare and contrast between aspects of a theme and moral didactic lessons that deeply engage the learner and those who yearned to learn. Therefore, it is not surprising that even the uneducated common people would attempt to learn and practise composing hanshi in private, due to its esteemed intellectual content that not only taught but admonished both the elite officials and common people through enlightenment. Hence, hanshi is more engaging. The content of later Choson still remained faithful to the tradition and tendency of poets to include rich nature imagery which was repeatedly expounded to reveal and describe in a parabolic manner the inner intentions of men, at times hideous, that escaped from being explicit, i.e. corrupt officials in the royal court. On the other hand, such imagery also added a blend of pure descriptions of beauty and admiration for the changing season, e.g. Hwang Hyon's "New Year's Eve" that is ironically melancholic and depressing, and how each season was trying to tell a particular aspect or story of one's life. Such rich and diversity of elements common in hanshi make it a time-defying literary and intellectual pleasure that engage the reader who finds interest in them.

In the "Song of Right and Wrong," Kim Sakkat engaged in a repetitive play of words of day, month and year, which was unfairly described as more of a folk humour. Looking more closely, this hanshi feigned underlying meaningful iteration of most people's lack of interest or boredom on the humdrum repetitiveness of each day, giving into months, and then years, or even decades. At least to the majority of the people, daily routine can be uneventful, similar and repeated in the same fashion of twelve hours each of daylight and nighttime, and Kim expressed this well in the literal sense. Following, the poem played with the words "right" and "wrong" again, which again might be a strategy of masking the skewed morals of corrupt royal officials, who presumed right in the face of wrong and unable to tell their differences apart. Such could be a moral remark on the injustice of court politics.

The Song of White Gull is another interesting literary strategy in which Kim employed the camouflaged effect of both the white gull and white sand. In an explicit sense, both have the same shade of colour and the sand cleverly hides the gull. However, looking intuitively, the white gull is a live being and a bird which connotates purity and innocence. Kim might be hinting the less noticeable pure and morally upright loyals of the king camouflaged amongst myriad of corrupt officals in the royal court, hence countless particles of white "non-living" sand, which at the sound or song of the authoritative fisherman, would bring the white gull to flight and be distinguished from unjust officials. Then, the next poem which talks about thirty guests going to forty houses and greedily asking for an extra serving of twenty more bowls of rice could be a depiction of bribery and corruption of the officials again. In "Presented to the Kisaeng," Kim talked about a destined encounter with a kisaeng who was presumably well-versed in poetry like him and how they were a well-matched pair under the moon, which associated action and destiny with symbolism. In "Lies," the content and elements employed are an ingenious application of how things, whether living or non-living, can be disproportionately magnified, distorted or skewed under the visual effects of changing amounts of light and darkness, but more so with greater proportions of darkness, hinting that truths and real nature are best seen under full light.

Hwang Hyon's hanshi somewhat bear a message that is more deeply emotional and touches on faithfulness and allegiance than the didactic ones of Kim Sakkat. Inevitably, due to the unstable period of later Choson, they are more depressing and melancholic that described separation and hopelessness. In "Seeing Yong-jae in dreams," Hwang talked about his sentimental longing and grieving for his good friend that never ceases like the winds and bamboos always blowing and rustling. Then, in "New Year's Eve," his insomnia and depression did not improve even with the advent of the new year. Intuitively, certain men in traditional times may prioritised same-gender loyal friendships and machoism more than their families and kinship. Although the stream was softly making way for spring, the water was still burdened and topped over with heavy snow of the winter season, which is a meaningful nature imagery. Another depressing "Putting an End to Myself(1) expressed the loss of a king to whom Hwang was loyal and his deserted palace, which ultimately removed his will to live.

In sasol shijo, we could see the authors applying the language, tone and positions of satirists and the common people. Therefore, these poems lack a posture and voice of politeness, refinement and calm introspection with consistent and well-organised thought structure of the educated. In sasol shijo No. 234, the content was filled with complaints and derogatory, at times figurative, remarks of a married woman's mother and father-in-laws and members of the in-law family, which was a striking contrast with the kasa, A Cautionary Song. It was chatty and crude-sounding, though frank with a commoner's impulsive wisdom. In sasol shijo No. 233, the content talked about a verbal interaction between a crab or seafood seller, presumably in an open marketplace, with a potential buyer, which is wordy and persistent in advertising his food products. It was again an unrefined verbal exchange between seemingly uneducated commoners with subtle comical effect or humour. In sasol shijo No. 235, the message it conveyed is that of a less knowledgeable daughter-in-law assured and advised by an easy-going mother-in-law who was slow to find fault with the girl. Although it is satirical, it nevertheless expressed the yearning and honesty of daughter-in-laws in olden times. Perhaps, due to the less conservative nature and attitude of the commoners who may not be educated and well-versed in moral etiquette and constraints taught by Confucianism or Neo-Confucianism, the structure and voice of sasol shijo are less consistent and filled with active and decisive verbal utterances of impulsively frank and swift-reacting common people. Therefore, they lack a proper pattern of teaching and expression that flows with progress. For this reason and others described above, hanshi is the genre that intensely engages readers who delight in Eastern traditional virtues, values, and refinement.

Figure 1: A symbol and connotation of white inner purity, innocence and integrity, the gull is frequently mentioned and expressed in hanshi by esteemed poets.

Literature: The Tale of Shim Ch'ong and Tears of Blood

"The Tale of Shim Ch'ong" (Pihl, 1994) is a story which comes with a number of paired major and secondary implicit and outward themes. First and foremost, its major theme is the admirable devotion and faithfulness of filial daughter Shim Ch'ong towards her father, Blindman Shim Hak-kyu. The story strongly emphasises the duties and responsibilities a daughter should bear towards her single disabled father, even to the point of death, as in the case when Shim Ch'ong had to give up her life to pay for her father's debt of promise to the monk, who ironically also rescued Shim Hak-kyu's life from the ditch. However, Shim Hak-kyu being visually impaired also leads to the implicit or intuitive theme of Shim Ch'ong being unable to take care of him in her absence after she would be forced against her will to leave him. On the other hand, a secondary outward theme is the importance of keeping one's word and promise, especially towards a person who has helped yourself, which in the case of Shim Hak-kyu, is the monk who promised restoration of eyesight with 300 sacks of rice and saved him from the ditch - a double honour. Yet, such an ideal moral code came at a huge price, for both Shim Ch'ong and her father, which ironically did not result in return of sight for Shim Hak-kyu - an implicit theme. Nevertheless, according to the author, such virtues in conflict may be necessary, though less important compared with his idea for the progress of the story's plot. The payment of a sacrifice of 300 sacks of rice with another inhumane sacrifice of daughter Shim Ch'ong may be regarded as inadequate, for the "Jade Emperor" saw through the hearts of the people and intervened for the sake of the filial girl. Perhaps, a less obvious or direct outward theme was the need and gratitude of the parents for their children. This brings us to the question of whether Shim Hak-kyu was seeing the restoration of his eyesight, the 300 sacks of sacrificial rice and his promise to the monk or Buddha to be more important than the presence and his kinship or companionship and need for Shim Ch'ong, at least over an instant of the moment when he confessed his problem to her. Could this imply that he was subconsciously hoping for her to help in any way possible, although not for a second thought that this would sacrifice her to the Dragon King? In addition, if he had known his daughter well enough and that she deeply treasured him, Shim Hak-kyu would not have rushed out of the house when she was late for home, knowing well enough that he was blind, only to fall into a ditch, and being emotionally aware that she would do all she could to obtain his 300 sacks of rice. The significance of these paired secondary outward and implicit themes is suggested by the fact that only when Shim Hak-kyu was determined to reunite with his daughter at the palace, though without much knowledge of her appearance, and that the most rewarding virtue of Shim Ch'ong's faithfulness to her father, even more than the king, being granted an opportunity, then we could finally see a perfect ending, almost like conflicted virtues being appeased and consolidated.

In Tears of Blood authored by Yi Injik (Yi & Skillend, 1989), the protagonist Ongnyon's determination to be a high achiever educated female in a world, whether Korea or Japan, that was witnessing and experiencing a transitional period from a traditional to a new modern society is an encompassing theme that travels through time and space. To be a well-educated female then was beginning to be highly esteemed in Japan, while Korea was at first slow to respond to such a change. Therefore, shortly after separation from her biological mother, Ongnyon was doing all the best she could in her daily life and education to please her adoptive Japanese mother in spite of the absence of Major Inoue who rescued and sent her to Japan. She might have temporarily forgotten about Korea and her biological parents. This brings us to the accompanying implicit theme of the virtue of devotion to one's real parents being challenged due to separation from them, that is in conflict with Ongnyon's earnest attempt to do her parents or guardian proud. On the other hand, while Ongnyon succeeded at first in pleasing her Japanese mother by fully adapting to the Japanese culture and language and meeting the demands of a foreign education, there is the secondary implicit theme of the reality that Mrs Inoue completely changed her attitude and former love for the child not long after the death of Major Inoue. This just reminds of another set of themes in the story which takes us back to the focus of Ongnyon's biological mother. Such virtues in conflict relate to the outward theme of the gain of the modern mindset of beliefs, knowledge and educational achievements which cause others to look up to and admire our efforts. This pairs with the implicit theme of deep emotional attachments one shares with a kin and loved ones, for in her moment of deepest despair and suicide, Ongnyon's biological mother reached out to her heart, foretold of her future and rescued her from attempts of death. Therefore, the author could have emphasised the positive values and effects of Japanese modernisation but it still became somewhat questionable when Ongnyon had to leave her adoptive mother and Japan. Perhaps, he was hinting for the people to take a better and more wholesome view of the world at large beyond Japan, such as the United States, and questioning to what extent Japanese modern values are entirely positive and beneficial given the temporal love which Mrs Inoue could afford Ongnyon, and that there are the essence and basic values of traditional Korea that are worthwhile to linger and carry on through subsequent new generations. It cannot be denied that through all the number of obstacles and challenges, the author's or Ongnyon's heart is to reunite with her mother ultimately in Korea, hence a part of the virtues in conflict since the beginning of their separation.

The story's themes therefore also revolve around a national and within-person conflict pertaining to Korea and the emerging educated female social class. The acceptance of modern and foreign influences is less so the question, when compared with the necessity for preservation of one's biological and culturally traditional roots. It is also a matter of evolution of identity of the Koreans, particularly the women, and how a seemingly conflicting "outwardly" Japanese or modern, and "inwardly" or biologically Korean individual could maintain a cooperative unitary mindset and system of modern life to pursue the benefits of progress and advancement of one's birth country.

Works Cited

Pihl, M. R. (1994). "The Song of Shim Ch'ŏng," *The Korean singer of tales*. Council on East Asian Studies.

O'Rourke, Kevin. (2006) *The Book of Korean Poetry: Songs of Shilla & Koryŏ*. Univ. of Iowa Press.

Yi, I., & Skillend, W. E. (1989). Tears of Blood. In *Korean Classical Literature: An Anthology* (pp. 63–63). essay, Kegan Paul International.

www.ingramcontent.com/pod-product-compliance
Lightning Source LLC
Chambersburg PA
CBHW082023050526

44107CB00101B/646